A Beginner's Guide to
DISABILITY INSURANCE CLAIMS
IN CANADA

How to Apply for and Win Payment of Disability Insurance Benefits, Even After a Denial or Unsuccessful Appeal

DAVID BRANNEN

Resolute Legal
A National Disability Benefits Law Firm
Toll Free: 1-800-480-9050
resolutelegal.ca

ISBN: 978-1-4834-2558-0 (sc)
ISBN: 978-1-4834-2557-3 (e)

Lulu Publishing Services rev. date: 01/29/2015

DAVID BRANNEN BIOGRAPHY

David Brannen is a disability claims lawyer and the founder of Resolute Legal. With headquarters in Moncton, New Brunswick, Resolute Legal is a national disability benefits law firm that serves Canadians who need to win payment of long-term disability benefits from insurance companies, or the Canada Pension Program (CPP), or both.

David was born in Brampton, Ontario. He grew up in Ontario and on Cape Sable Island, a beautiful fishing community in Southwestern Nova Scotia. He now lives in Dieppe, New Brunswick with his wife, two step children, and dog Penny.

David has a unique professional background that makes him uniquely qualified work in the area of disability claims. Before becoming a lawyer David obtained a Master of Science Degree in Occupational Therapy from Dalhousie University in Halifax, Nova Scotia. Before becoming a lawyer, David worked as a licensed occupational therapist in Nova Scotia, New Brunswick and the United States.

David graduated from the Schulich School of Law at Dalhousie University in 2004. In addition to earing his law degree, David also obtained a diploma in Health Law and Policy from the Dalhousie Health Law Institute.

David worked as a personal injury law for eight years at a large personal injury law firm before leaving to start Resolute Legal in 2013. David continues to act as co-counsel on some personal injury cases, but focuses almost exclusively on representing Canadians who need to win payment of long-term disability benefits from insurance companies or the CPP disability program.

CONTENTS

INTRODUCTION

Anyone applying for disability insurance benefits in Canada faces an uphill battle. There is a good chance that your insurance company will either deny your claim, or stop payment of benefits, *even if you are truthful and legitimately disabled*. Understanding *how* and *why* insurance representatives deny legitimate disability claims is your key to success.

To have any hope of winning payment of disability benefits, you need to fully appreciate *the claims adjuster's dilemma*. Insurance companies are in business to make a profit. Everyone in the company is incentivized to increase profits. Your disability claim – if approved – reduces profits. Your claims adjuster knows that if he approves your claim, internal auditors and managers will scrutinize his decision. He knows he better get it right – approving a claim that auditors feel *should have been denied* is career suicide at an insurance company.

Claims adjusters are under tremendous pressure to deny any claim – including legitimate claims –*for which a plausible argument can be made in favour of denial*. This is why your disability claim may be denied even though you are legitimately disabled.

If you are like most people, you will prepare a *bare minimum claim*, which includes only the forms the insurance company gives you. This type of claim is usually full of holes and loose ends that – for all practical purposes – *requires the adjuster to deny your claim*. By submitting a weak claim, you have made it impossible for the adjuster to approve it (if he wants to keep his job), even if he believes you are disabled and deserving of benefits.

So what does it take to get the adjuster to approve your claim? You need to go beyond the *bare minimum* and submit a claim that is comprehensive, persuasive, and includes overwhelming evidence in favour of approval. I call this *the winning claim*. When the adjuster receives such a claim he will breath a sigh of relief. This is a claim he can approve without fear of being overruled by auditors and managers. He won't have to worry about losing his Christmas bonus. He can approve your claim with confidence and move on to denying other peoples' claims that are no so well put together.

So how do you prepare *a winning claim*? In the pages that follow I give you the exact process that many top disability lawyers in Canada and the United States use to win payment of disability benefits cases. I show you step-by-step the process Resolute Legal uses to build a *winning claim* at all stages of the process, including the initial claim for benefits; during appeals of benefit denials; and, in lawsuits for payment of benefits. By following this process, you will give yourself the maximum chance of success.

Be forewarned. The process for preparing a *winning claim* is not easy. It takes more time than preparing a *bare minimum claim*. It costs more money. It also involves specialized knowledge and judgment that must be applied on a case-by-case basis, taking into account your occupation, your medical condition and your insurance company. A one-size-fits-all approach is doomed to fail.

If you plan to apply for disability benefits on your own, or are in the process of doing so, it is essential that you take time to educate yourself about the entire disability claims process. This book includes much of the background information you need to know. This knowledge will allow you to avoid making common mistakes that will guarantee a denial of your claim. If you choose to hire a lawyer, this book gives guidance on how a lawyer may be able to help you, and identifies red flags you should watch for, so you can avoid getting ripped off.

CHAPTER 1

What Are Disability Insurance Benefits?

In this chapter:

- What type of disability plan do you have?
- What are the types of disability benefits?
- What is a disability benefits claim?

What Type of Disability Plan Do You Have?

It is important for you to figure out what type of disability plan you have. The type of plan you have will dictate the rules that apply to you; your obligations; and, the strategy you want to use. Generally speaking, there are two types of disability plans: 1) Insurance-based disability plans and 2) Non-profit disability plans.

The vast majority of disability benefits plans in Canada are insurance-based disability plans. These include group disability insurance policies offered as part of employee benefit packages and individual disability policies sold directly to professionals or self-employed business people.

Non-profit disability plans are different because they are not based on an insurance policy. An employer normally runs these plans for their own employees or the disability plan is run by a non-profit board of directors, for the benefit of a group of employees. While there is no insurance policy, the rules of the disability plan are set out in a document called the "Plan Text" and it reads just like an insurance policy, and has the same types of clauses and language.

On the outside looking in, non-profit disability plans look and feel like disability insurance plans. This is because employers and the non-profit boards hire insurance companies to administer the plan for them. This leads people to think the insurance company administering the plan is also providing the benefits, which technically it is not. In these situations the insurance company is only an agent or middleman. This only becomes important if you bring a lawsuit for payment of benefits. You would need to sue the employer or non-profit board, rather than in insurance company.

Group Disability Insurance Policies

Group disability insurance policies are the most common type of disability insurance plan in Canada. Having group disability insurance means that you are insured as part of a group, as opposed to buying your own personal insurance policy. The group shares a common *sponsor*, which is usually an employer, professional organization, union, or bank. The sponsor buys the group insurance policy from the insurance company for the benefit of the sponsor's members (i.e., you).

Your disability insurance is likely part of a group insurance plan if one of the following situations applies to you:

- You get your disability insurance benefits through your employment.
- You get your disability insurance benefits from membership in an organization (e.g., professional association, union, Chamber of Commerce).
- You pay for disability insurance on a loan (e.g., mortgages, car loans, lines of credit).

Group disability insurance policies can provide both short-term and long-term disability benefits. You will have to read your group insurance benefits booklet to see if your group plan includes both short- and long-term disability benefits.

Non-profit Disability Benefits Plans

Many people who work for public sector organizations (provincial governments; regional health authorities, etc.), or are members of public sector unions, have disability benefits through non-profit disability benefits plans. These plans are funded by payments made by employee-members and the employer. The money is held in a trust fund and is governed and administered by a board of trustees or committee.

The boards of trustees often hire insurance companies to administer the benefits plan under administrative services only (ASO) agreements. An ASO agreement means that the insurance company is only administering the plan and is not providing the insurance policy; however, because the insurance company becomes the front-line administrator, this leads to confusion, as plan members sometimes believe that they have a group insurance policy with the insurance company.

Non-profit disability benefits plans differ from disability insurance plans in a few important ways:

- It is common for non-profit disability plans to have more comprehensive rehabilitation and internal appeals procedures.
- Non-profit disability plans often have shorter deadlines, which are more strictly enforced.
- Many non-profit disability plans have mandatory internal appeal procedures (these are optional under insurance plans).
- Under some non-profit disability plans, you may not have the right to file a lawsuit if the plan denies your benefits.
- Under some non-profit disability plans, you have to choose whether to use the internal appeals process the lawsuit process.

If you determine you have disability benefits through a non-profit disability plan, then you should seek legal advice immediately, as you may be dealing with shorter deadlines; more complex benefits procedures; and greater restrictions on your legal rights.

Individual Disability Insurance Policies

Individual disability insurance policies are the least common type of disability insurance plan; they are sold to self-employed people, including professionals, tradespeople, executives, and business owners.

To have this type of insurance policy, you would have had to buy it directly from an insurance broker. The policy itself would be issued by a disability insurance company and would cover you as long as you pay the monthly premiums.

The important features of individual disability polices are as follows:

- You will have a more rigorous application process than what is typical with other plans.
- The insurance company will carefully analyze the forms you signed and filled out when you bought the policy (to try and void your policy for misrepresentation).
- You will have to provide personal and corporate tax records, along with data about your professional practice over the past few years.

Individual insurance policies can offer a wide range of benefits, depending on whether you bought a no-frills policy or a Cadillac policy.

What Are The Types Of Disability Benefits

Paid Sick Leave

Some employers provide paid sick leave benefits in addition to short-term disability benefits. Usually you only have several days of paid sick leave, but in some cases you may have weeks or months of "banked" sick time available to them.

You should not delay submitting your application for disability insurance benefits just because you are being paid sick leave benefits. Many people wrongly assume that they should wait to apply for disability insurance benefits until after exhausting all sick leave benefits. This is a big mistake.

There are deadlines to apply for disability benefits. You can easily miss a deadline to apply for benefits while you are still being paid with banked sick leave benefits. Many employers are unaware of these deadlines and will not warn you about them, or even worse they will tell you to delay your application for disability benefits until the sick leave benefits are exhausted.

Employment Insurance Sickness Benefits

If you don't have short-term disability benefits, and have less than 15 weeks of paid sick leave, then you will want to apply for employment insurance (EI) sickness benefits as soon as possible. Service Canada's website (www.servicecanada.gc.ca) has information about EI sickness benefits, and you can download the application forms from their website. You can apply online for EI sickness benefits, but you will still need to get a medical report from your doctor and a Record of Employment (ROE) from your employer. Service Canada will not process your application for EI sickness benefits until it has received your medical report and the ROE from your employer.

Short-Term Disability Benefits

Short-term disability benefits are often (but not always) included as part of a group disability benefits plan. As the name suggests, short-term disability benefits are meant to provide you with disability benefits for short absences from work because of illness or disability.

Short-term disability benefits provide weekly or bi-weekly income payments for a few months. You normally have to use up all your sick days before you become eligible for short-term disability benefits. The payment amount is a percentage of your base salary (e.g., 60 percent, of pre-disability weekly earnings) or a specific amount (e.g., $500 per week). The specific payment amounts or percentages are set out in your insurance policy. The benefit period (maximum time you can receive payments) is usually between three and six months.

Long-Term Disability Benefits

Long-term disability benefits provide monthly income payments during longer absences from the workplace. To become eligible to receive benefits, you must be out of work continuously for a specific minimum time (e.g., three to six months). Insurance companies refer to this minimum time the "waiting period" or "elimination period."

Long-term disability monthly payments are a percentage of your salary (e.g., 60 to 70 percent of salary) or a specific monthly amount (e.g., $2,000 per month), or a combination of both (e.g., benefits are 66 percent of monthly salary, up to a maximum of $4,000 per month). The exact amounts or percentages are found in your insurance policy. The benefit period (maximum time you can receive benefits) can be a certain number of years (e.g., 2, 5, or 10 years) or until you reach a certain age (e.g., 60, 65, or 67), or a combination of both (e.g., a maximum of 10 years or to age 65).

What is a Disability Benefits Claim?

If you have disability insurance and you become disabled because of an accident or illness, then you likely have the right to apply for payment of disability benefits under the insurance policy. This is called "making or filing a claim for benefits."

The purpose of insurance is to protect you from risks that are known but may not happen. Almost everyone understands the concept of home insurance. You agree to pay a monthly premium, and in return the insurance company agrees to pay you in the event that your home accidently burns down.

Disability insurance is similar to home insurance. Home insurance protects you against the risk of accidentally losing your home to fire. Disability insurance protects you against accidentally losing your ability to work or earn income.

CHAPTER 2

How to Know If You Are Eligible to Apply for Disability Insurance Benefits

In this chapter:

- Are you enrolled in a disability benefits plan?
- What is the enrollment probation period?
- Did you suffer an "accident" or "illness"?
- Did you suffer a workplace accident?
- Do you have a pre-existing condition?

Even if you have disability insurance, you still must be eligible to apply for benefits. Disability insurance plans do not apply in every situation. In addition to being unable to work, there are other conditions you must meet in order to qualify to apply for disability benefits.

Are You Enrolled in a Disability Benefits Plan?

Most people in Canada are not eligible to apply for disability insurance benefits. You can only be eligible for disability benefits if you are enrolled in a disability income benefits plan. Do not assume you have disability insurance benefits just because you have group insurance benefits through your work. Many group benefits plans cover medical expenses, dental expenses, and life insurance but don't provide disability benefits.

What Is the Enrollment Probation Period?

If you become disabled after recently enrolling in a group benefits plan, it is important to determine if you have passed the probation period to apply for disability insurance benefits. Most disability insurance policies include a probationary period of a few months following your initial enrollment. This means the policy will not cover any disability that arises during the probationary period. This rule is intended to prevent people from running out and buying insurance once they believe they may be sick or will become disabled. The exact duration of the probationary period is listed in each policy.

Did You Suffer an "Accident" or "Illness"?

It is important to understand that the cause of your disability will be an important factor in determining if you are eligible to make a claim for disability insurance benefits. Each insurance policy or plan is different, so it is important to read your own benefits booklet to see what causes of disability are covered. For example, some policies will only cover disability arising from "accidents," but others will also cover disability arising from "accidents or illness." Disability arising from suicide attempts may not be covered by disability insurance. Some risky behaviours like skydiving may not be covered.

Keep in mind that the terms "accident" and "illness" have unique meanings within the context of disability insurance policies. The meaning of these words within insurance policies is more nuanced than the ordinary meanings of these words. These phases have a long history of being interpreted by courts. It is important for you to consult a lawyer experienced in disability insurance law to help determine if your situation constitutes an "accident" or "illness" as defined by your insurance policy.

Did You Suffer a Workplace Accident?

Workplace accidents are sometimes not covered by disability insurance. Or if they are covered, the insurance company gets to deduct the payments you are entitled to receive from your province's worker's compensation program. Courts have interpreted "entitled to receive" to include situations where a person could have applied for worker's compensation benefits, but chose not to do so. It is very important that you apply for worker's compensation benefits if there is any possibility your disability could be caused by a "workplace accident."

Do You Have a Pre-Existing Condition?

Most disability insurance policies and plans have pre-existing condition exclusions. The wording of the pre-existing condition exclusions differs from policy-to-policy, but they usually kick-in when you have been enrolled in the disability plan for less than a year. In other words, if you have started a new job and join the group disability plan, you can't make a disability claim under the plan for a condition for which you received medical treatment in the past few months or over the last year.

If you have been enrolled in your disability plan or policy for a number of years, then this exclusion will likely not apply, even if you have had treatment for the condition over a number of years. The purpose of these pre-existing condition exclusions is to prevent a person from signing up for disability plan when the person is already disabled, or soon will be.

CHAPTER 3

How to Find and Understand the Specifics of Your Disability Benefits Plan

In this chapter:

- What does it mean to be "totally disabled"?
- When do my monthly benefits start?
- How much are my monthly benefits?
- If I qualify for benefits, how long will I get them?
- Do I pay income tax on my monthly benefits?

Most disability insurance plans require the insurance company to pay monthly benefits if you become "totally disabled". The definition of "totally disabled," the amount of the payment, when the payment starts, and how long it is paid can vary widely from plan to plan.

The rules that apply to you will be found in your disability insurance policy or plan text. Your employer or insurance company will often summarize the rules in a group benefits booklet. It is often difficult for you to get a copy of the actual policy or plan text without the help of a lawyer.

What Does It Mean to Be "Totally Disabled"?

The definition of "total disability" is different from plan to plan, so you must read your own plan documents to understand how it is defined in your situation. Generally speaking, total disability means that you are unable to work or hold down a job.

Your disability plan may have more than one definition of total disability. It is very common for plans to define total disability for the first 24 months to mean the inability to do your own occupation at the time you became disabled. After 24 months, the definition of total disability changes to mean that you must be unable to do any occupation.

The precise definition of "any occupation" is different in each insurance policy; however, the Supreme Court of Canada has ruled that, no matter the precise wording, the concept of "any occupation" does not literally mean *any* occupation. The alternate occupation must be suitable based on a number of factors, including your age, education, and work experience.

When Do My Monthly Benefits Start?

Every disability benefit plan will set out a "benefit start date." This is the first day that you can qualify to receive disability benefits. The start date is calculated using your last day of work. You disability insurance plan will set out a waiting period of three to six months that starts the day following your last day at work. Your benefit start date is the day after the end of the waiting period.

How Much Are My Monthly Benefits?

The amount of your monthly benefits will be found in your disability policy or plan. It will be either a specific dollar amount (e.g., $4,000 per month) or expressed as a formula (e.g., 66 percent of your base monthly salary). The exact dollar amounts and percentages differ from policy to policy and from plan to plan.

If I Qualify for Benefits, How Long Will I Get Them?

How long benefits are paid is called the "benefit period." The length of the benefit period can vary widely from plan to plan. The benefit period is set out in your disability plan. It will be until you reach a certain age (usually age 65), or it can be for a certain number of years, or a combination of both.

Do I Pay Income Tax On Monthly Benefits

Your disability benefits may or may not be taxable as income. It will depend on the type of disability plan you have and what percentage of the monthly premium you pay and what percentage your employer pays. If you pay the full premium, then benefits are not taxable. If you and your employer both pay a percentage of the premium, then you will need to give the plan careful analysis to determine if your benefits are taxable. Sometimes the insurance plan or policy will set out the taxation status of the benefits: Taxable or non-taxable.

C H A P T E R 4

How to Prepare a Winning Application for Short- or Long-term Disability Benefits

In this chapter:

- What do I have to prove?
- What should I do before getting the claim forms?
- How to prepare a "bare minimum" claim
- How to prepare a "winning claim"

What Do I Have To Prove?

To prove your disability claim you need to establish three things: 1) you have an illness or injury; 2) the illness or injury has reduced your functional capacity; 3) as a result of your reduced functional capacity, you are unable to meet the occupational standard specified in your disability policy or plan text.

The Definition of Disability

To win benefits you have to prove that you are "disabled" as defined by your specific insurance policy or plan text. There is no standard definition of disability. Each policy or benefits plan has its own specific definition of disability. This is why it's critical to get your hands on a copy of your disability policy or plan text. Otherwise you won't know exactly what you have to prove.

Most policies and plans will define disability something like this: "due to illness or injury the person is unable to perform the substantial duties of his or her own occupation"

"Own" Occupation vs. "Any" Occupation

It is common for disability insurance policies to have two definitions of disability. There will be an initial short period where disability will be defined as the inability to do the substantial duties of your "own" occupation. Then after the initial period (usually 12 to 24 months), the definition of disability will change to the inability to do the substantial duties of "any" occupation reasonably suited to you given your age, education and experience"

It is harder to prove you can't do the substantial duties of "any" occupation (as compared to your "own" occupation), so it is common for insurance companies to stop payment of benefits at the point where the definition of disability changes from "own" occupation to "any" occupation. This is called the disability-definition changeover.

Insurance companies track the disability-definition-changeover date very carefully. They will do everything possible to build a case against you so they can stop payment after the initial "own" occupation period. This is because it is harder for you to prove you can't do "any" occupation as compared to your "own" occupation.

A Doctor Saying You Are Disabled, Is Not Proof You Are Disabled

You cannot prove you are disabled simply by getting your doctor to say so. This is where many doctors, claimants and lawyers go wrong. They wrongfully believe that the insurance company "must" approve the claim if a doctor says the person is disabled from work.

Courts have held that a doctor saying someone is disabled is just one fact to be considered. Unless the doctor explains in detail why he or she concludes you are disabled, insurance companies and judges will not give the doctor's opinion much credit.

Your insurance company has it own doctors working behind-the-scenes. You never meet these doctors, but they are reviewing every report and letter sent in by your doctor. These behind-the-scenes doctors are very experienced with disability claims. They pick apart what your doctor is saying and try to make your doctor look incompetent.

Winning CPP Disability Benefits Is Not Proof You Are Disabled

Many people and inexperienced lawyers wrongfully believe that winning CPP disability benefits is "proof" you are disabled and, therefore, the insurance company "must" pay your benefits.

Disability insurance companies and plan administrators are not required to follow the decisions of the CPP disability administration. While winning CPP disability benefits certainly doesn't hurt your chances of winning disability insurance benefits, winning CPP disability benefits is not conclusive proof of disability.

To use a sports analogy, it is important to appreciate that insurance companies and the CPP disability administration are in different leagues. CPP disability is the minor leagues and insurance companies are in the major leagues. In other words, insurance companies will put a hundred times more effort and money into proving you are not disabled than will the CPP disability administration. In fact, it is very common that the insurance company will have much more negative information and evidence against you. In many cases, if the CPP disability administration had all the information your insurance company had (surveillance videos, insurance company doctor reports, etc), it would also have denied your claim!

What Should I Do Before Getting The Claim Forms?

You make a claim for disability benefit by completing the application forms required under your disability policy or plan. Your Policy or Plan will tell you the exact forms you need to fill out and return to them for your application to be "complete".

It is important to submit all the forms quickly because the insurance company does not have to review or consider "incomplete" applications. Your application will be "incomplete" until all forms are returned to them, so a delay of one form will delay your entire application.

You can get the forms from your employer or human resources department; however, it is usually a big mistake to start the process of applying for disability benefits by asking for the forms. There are actually many things you need to do before you even ask for the forms.

Following are my recommended steps you should take *before you ask for the disability claim forms*:

Step 1: Read Your Group Benefits Booklet

One of the first things you need to do is get (and read) your group benefits booklet. This seems like common sense, but most people have not seen their disability insurance booklet or insurance policy, and the only information they have is what the insurance company representatives have told them in letters and emails.

You get the group benefits booklet from your group benefits plan sponsor, which will be your employer, union, or professional organization. Most often they will give you a paper booklet, but sometimes this information is only available online, so they may direct you to a website

Once you have your benefits booklet (or have found the online information), read through it and try to answer the following questions:

- Do I have short-term disability benefits? If yes, how much is paid per week? What is the maximum number of days or weeks paid?
- What is the waiting period for long-term disability benefits?
- What is the formula for calculating the long-term disability monthly payment amount?
- What is the benefit period for long-term disability benefits? Is it a specific number of years (i.e., two, five, or ten), or is it payable to a certain age (i.e., age sixty-five), or is it some combination of both (e.g., payable for five years or to age sixty-five, whichever happens first).
- What is the definition of total disability?
- Is there an "own occupation" clause? If so, how is it defined?
- How many months or years will the occupation criteria apply?
- Is there an "any occupation" clause? If so, how is it defined?
- Are there any other restrictions on payment of benefits?

Step 2: Create an Exit Strategy For Leaving Work

Choosing the day to stop working is one of the most important decisions you will make. Most people give this no thought at all and just stop working on any random day. Picking the wrong day can guarantee your claim will be denied and can make it very difficult for you to win at court, even if you are legitimately disabled.

Warning: *Do not quit or allow yourself to be fired before you apply for disability insurance benefits.* Most people lose the ability to work gradually over time due to chronic illness or injuries. As your disability worsens, your work also suffers. Some employers will be compassionate, but others will simply view you as lazy or a bad employee. If you are working in a toxic workplace, you may face discrimination because of your disability. It is natural you may reach a breaking point where you simply quit your job on the spur of the moment. Or worse, you see the warning signs that your employer is preparing to fire you, or to lay you off because of your disability.

It is critical that you apply for disability benefits before you quit or are fired or laid off. You are only eligible to make a disability claim while you are *employed* and *actively at work*.

Finally, please understand that you will only qualify for disability benefits if you can prove that you far exceed the definition of "total disability" found in your policy. Every insurance policy or plan has a different definition. Therefore, it is critical that you not stop working until you are confident that you can get *evidence* to show that you far exceed the insurance company's criteria.

If the insurance company denies your application, its lawyer will carefully examine and question why you chose to stop working on the day you did. This can become difficult to answer if you worked for weeks and months up to the day you went off work. You need to make sure your medical records show that you had a gradual decline over time and justify your decision to stop working on the day you did.

Step 3: Confirm You Have Your Doctor's Support

It is critical that you not stop working until your doctor supports your decision to do so. The insurance company will never approve claims for people who do not have full support from their family doctor. Remember, they will likely deny your claim even if your doctor supports, you, and so if your doctor is not supportive, or is just neutral, then you have no chance of winning disability benefits.

What do you do if your doctor doesn't agree that you are unable to work due to disability? This is a difficult situation that you need to handle very carefully. Understand that doctors are human, and there is a wide range of competence, attitudes, and biases between individual doctors. You have a few options depending on why you believe the doctor is not supportive of you:

Your doctor needs more convincing. With chronic illness, it is hard to say when it becomes unreasonable for someone to keep working. It is hard for a doctor to know when you cross the line from being reasonably able to work in discomfort to it being unreasonable for you to work. Sometimes, all that is needed is for you to show to the doctor that you have done all you can do to remain employed. A lawyer experienced with disability benefits cases can give you examples of how you can show your doctor that you have done all you can do. There is no dishonesty or trickery involved.

Your doctor is incompetent or biased. If you truly believe you cannot work much longer, and have taken steps to show your doctor you have done all you can do, and your doctor still doesn't support you, then you need to get a new doctor.

There is a wide range in competence and attitudes between doctors in Canada. Just because your current doctor doesn't support you, does not mean your case is hopeless. Doctors may lack an understanding of certain illnesses or conditions, or they may simply be biased or prejudiced against anyone who applies for disability benefits. Such doctors are rare, but I have certainly encountered them in my law practice, and they create problems for their disabled patients.

Changing doctors should always be the last resort and only done after you are satisfied that you have really done all you can do to show the doctor you legitimately cannot keep working.

Step 4: Make Arrangements with Your Employer

Once you have informed your employer you can't work because of disability, and have a medical note from your doctor confirming this, your job will be protected under provincial labour laws and human rights codes. From a legal point of view, there is a big difference between resigning (or quitting) your job and having to take a leave of absence from work for medical reasons. While on medical leave, you are still "employed". Keeping your status of employed will allow you to continue to use your medical and dental plan, pension plan, and other workplace benefits. Your employer may need more details from your doctor confirming your disability from work. Your employer also has the right to have you examined by its own doctor.

How To Prepare a "Bare Minimum" Claim

You apply for disability benefits by filling out a series of forms provided by the insurance company or plan administrator. Most disability insurance companies and plans in Canada use the same three basic forms: 1) Notice of Claim Form; 2) Employer's Report Form; and 3) Attending Physician's Report Form. Each insurance company's forms are slightly different, in terms of the layout and the questions asked, but they are basically all the same. By law, the insurance company must approve or deny your application based on the information included in these forms.

Disability insurance policies and plans have specific rules for the "bare minimum" you must do to submit a "complete application". If you don't submit a "complete application", then the insurance company doesn't even have to consider it, and they legally don't have to pay disability benefits to you, no matter how legitimately disabled you are.

In my experience, ninety-five percent of people filing claims for disability insurance benefits use what I call the "bare minimum" approach to filing a claim. This is unfortunate because the "bare minimum" approach has virtually no chance of success for many legitimately disabled people. As I have mentioned throughout this book, you need to present overwhelming evidence of your disability and this is impossible to do with a "bare minimum" approach.

Following is a review of the "bare minimum" you must do when filing a claim for disability benefits:

You Must Complete and Sign the "Notice of Claim Form"

The Notice of Claim Form is a standard form that all disability insurance companies require as part of an application for disability benefits. Each insurance company's form is slightly different, but they all ask for the same basic information. Many people fill out this form without giving it much thought. That is a major mistake. Common mistakes people make include providing improper descriptions of their illness or injury and providing incorrect dates for onset of disability and the last day of work.

You Must Arrange for Your Employer to Complete and Sign the "Employer's Report Form"

All insurance companies will require your employer to fill out a form with information about your employment. This form asks the employer for your job title, rate of pay, annual salary and other descriptions about your work duties. It is your responsibility to arrange for your employer to fill out this form. You must then get it from your employer and send it to the insurance company, or arrange for the employer to send it to them.

You Must Arrange for Your Doctor to Complete and Sign the "Attending Physician's Report Form"

All insurance companies will require a report from your doctor (i.e., physician). This form is called the "Attending Physician's Report Form." It is your responsibility to make sure you doctor fills out the form properly. You must also arrange for the doctor to send the completed form to the insurance company, or you have to pick it up from the doctor and send it yourself. You are also responsible to pay any fee the doctor charges for filling out this form.

Phone Interview with Insurance Representative

While it is technically not a mandatory part of the application process, most insurance claims adjusters will want to do a detailed phone interview with you once they receive all your application forms. I usually recommend that people do this phone interview, but you need to approach it with extreme caution.

You need to be realistic about the purpose of the initial phone interview. The primary purpose of this call is for the insurance representative to troll for more information about you that he or she can use to justify denying your application. By the time this call happens, the insurance adjuster will have reviewed your application forms and identified facts or things that will make it difficult for them to deny the claim. He or she will then use the phone interview to try to get you to say things that will help them spin the "bad facts" (from their perspective) to be better in their favour, or at least make them neutral, so it is easier for them to deny the claim.

So why would you ever do this interview? If done properly, you can use this interview to your advantage. You need to know how to avoid the traps laid by the insurance adjuster and give information that will strengthen your case and make it harder for the insurance representative to deny your claim.

How to Prepare a "Winning Claim"

Everyone has to do the bare minimum (as described above) when applying for disability insurance benefits. The problem is that the vast majority of people (up to ninety-five percent in my experience) don't go any further than doing the "bare minimum". This is why so many legitimately disabled people have their claims denied by insurance companies.

If you are serious about winning payment of disability benefits, and want to avoid denials, appeals and delays, then you need to go beyond the "bare minimum" approach, and prepare what I call a "winning claim" for disability benefits.

Of course, no approach can guarantee all people will win, all of the time, but in my experience your chances of winning are vastly improved by using the approach I describe below.

Think of it this way. Picture the insurance adjuster sitting at his or her desk with stacks of insurance claims. The practical reality is that the adjuster can only approve a few of those claims. In this way, your claim is in a battle against all the other peoples' claims on the adjuster's desk. This isn't how it is supposed to work, but it is how things work in reality. So, to win, you need your claim to standout from the rest. You need to make it as hard as possible for the adjuster to deny your claim. You want them to approve your claim and move on to denying the other claims (that while they may be legitimate) are not as well-put-together as your claim, and offer more opportunities for the adjuster to find holes he or she can rely on to make a denial.

Following is the process I use to prepare a "winning claim":

Supplement Your "Notice of Claim Form"

You need to take great care when filling out the Notice of Claim Form. This form is the foundation of your claim for disability benefits. It is important that all information is 100% accurate. Even honest mistakes can later be used to make you look like a lair.

One of the strange things about the Notice of Claim Form is that it asks you for very important information about your diagnosis, your symptoms, your disability, limitations, and your work, *but only gives you a very small space to fill in your information.* If you only use this form (like ninety-five percent of claimants), you are doing yourself a big disservice. It is impossible to effectively provide complete information about your illness, disability, and employment on the one-page form they give you.

In addition to the Notice of Claim Form, *you need to provide a supplemental written statement that provides a persuasive narrative about your disability.* This statement needs to go into great detail about the progression of your disability in the years leading up to your last day of work. It needs to describe your job duties and then explain how your disability interfered with your ability to do those duties. You need to explain why you could work the day before you stopped working, but not afterwards. You need to explain why your medical condition is disabling for you, but not for many other people with the same medical diagnosis. You should discuss what a typical day looks like for you. You need to explain the steps you have taken to get better and to try and remain at work.

For maximum impact, you can provide this supplemental written statement in the form of a sworn affidavit. This is an advanced tactic that can give you a big advantage. A sworn affidavit shows the insurance company you are willing to stand by what you are saying. This can work in your favour; however, if you are not careful with how you prepare your affidavit, it could blow up in your face. You need to make sure your statements cannot be turned against you. Or that you make a statement the insurance company can argue isn't true. I do not recommend using a sworn affidavit without guidance from an experienced disability benefits lawyer.

Get Copies of All Your Medical Records

While I often see claimants who have copies of various medical letters written by a doctor, or a copy of a diagnostic imaging report, it is rare to see a claimant gathering complete medical files from all their doctors and other treatment professionals. This is a big mistake.

Once of the first things I do when hired on a disability claim, is to get complete copies of the family doctor's medical file, along with the files of any other key treatment providers (physiotherapists, psychiatrist, psychologist, etc). You are playing with fire when you fill out claim forms and give statements to the insurance company, while not knowing exactly what is said about you in your medical records. I can guarantee you there are things in there you don't expect.

Doctors and others often write down their impressions of what you told them during the visit. You need to make sure what you say is consistent with what is in the medical records. Otherwise, if there are inconsistences between what the doctor's records say you said, and what you are saying now, the insurance company can make it look like you are hiding something or are a liar.

Finally, in many cases, the complete medical records go along way to helping you show the seriousness of your disability. Often your doctors or other treatment providers will make notes about how you have struggled with work. Or how you have struggled with other activities of daily living. These types of records are very powerful in your favour and help show a complete picture of your situation.

If you have done the "bare minimum" application, and all the insurance company has is the medical form from your doctor, you are missing a big opportunity to help improve your chances of winning.

Give Your Doctor Guidance On How to Complete the Attending Physician's Report

Most people simply ask their doctor to complete the Attending Physician's Report Form without giving the doctor any type of guidance. If you assume doctors know how to effectively fill out insurance forms, then I am sorry, but you are seriously mistaken.

Poorly done Attending Physician Reports are probably the number one reason your claim will be denied. Even well meaning doctors, who believe you are disabled, can fill out the Form in a way that will guarantee a denial by the insurance company.

In fact, if the doctor simply follows the instructions on most of these Attending Physician Report Forms, they will produce a report that supports a denial of your claim. This happens because these forms often don't ask the doctor's the right questions that would produce answers and information that is favourable to you! Rather, these forms often ask the doctors to make general statements about your diagnosis and prognosis. Then when the doctor doesn't say much about your disability or ability to work, the insurance company will deny your claim for lack of medical evidence of disability.

Another common problem is that many doctors will simply say: "my patient is unable to work at this time". You might think that is great! But insurance companies will not see it that way. Bald statements such as this, without your doctor backing it up with analysis and reasoning, will not convince the insurance company to approve your claim. The insurance company will almost always have a doctor working behind-the-scenes to review your doctor's report and give a contrary opinion.

It is beyond the scope of this book for me to give you the exact process for how we at Resolute Legal provide guidance to doctors. This is because the guidance needs to be customized on a case-by-case basis, taking into account your specific medical condition and employment. It also has to take into account what your doctor and others have already said about your disability. We have our own forms we send to doctors that are customized in this way.

Review Your Employer's Report to Make Sure it is Accurate

If you are doing a "bare minimum" application, you will simply ask your supervisor or human resources department to fill out the Employers Report Form and then send it to the insurance company. This is a huge mistake.

After poorly done medical report forms, the second biggest problem I see is inaccurate information in the Employer's Report. The insurance company is relying on the Employer's Report to understand the physical and mental demands of your job.

Please heed my warning that you absolutely cannot trust your employer to accurately describe your job demands and duties. The person filling out the form may simply attach the company's standard employment description for your job, which may be outdated and make your job seem easier than it is. It is actually quite common for an employee's actual job demands and duties to be different from the official job description.

Also, employers and your supervisors or managers may have their own agendas. I have seen employers and employer representative intentionally put misleading information on the employer statement forms. This can happen if you were doing work you officially weren't supposed to be doing, or if you were doing undocumented overtime.

When getting the Employer's Report for my clients, I ask the employer to fill out the form and then return it to me. I then review it in detail with my client. If my client disagrees with anything the employer has written, I prepare a letter to the employer asking them to revise the Employer's Report. Most often the employer has made an honest mistakes and are more than willing to do the revisions. If they refuse to do the revisions, then I attach a rebuttal statement from my client along with the completed Employers Report. Without this type of oversight, you will be stuck with the employer's version of you what your job involves, even if it is not true.

Get Your Own Testing and Assessments to Verify Your Medical Condition or Disability

Do you want to know the secret to winning your disability claim? This is the tactic that top disability lawyers use to achieve much higher success rates than other people. The answer is to pay for your own medical testing and assessments.

The type of assessment or testing that would maximize your chances of success needs to be determined on a case-by-case basis. This decision would need to take into account: 1) your occupation; 2) your illness; and 3) the insurance company you are dealing with.

Examples of tests and assessments include, functional capacity evaluations, functional abilities assessments, neuropsychological testing, transferable skills assessments, examinations by specialist physicians, and vocational expert assessments.

These assessments provide direct opinions on your actual abilities (both physical and mental) from people who are qualified to give such opinions. Contrary to what you may believe, doctors are really not qualified to give opinions on your functional abilities or ability to work at a particular job.

The key to winning your disability claim is make sure the insurance claim file is full of overwhelming evidence of disability. In many cases, it is nearly impossible to build overwhelming evidence without paying for your own medical testing and assessments.

The difficulty with getting your own testing and assessments is that you have to pay for these yourself. These tests usually cost into the thousands of dollars. Unfortunately, Medicare does not cover these tests and assessments because they are not essential to your medical care. Disability lawyers will typically pay the cost of these assessments when your case is at the lawsuit stage; however, at the initial claim stage you would have to pay for these out of your own pocket.

Get Your Doctor to Write a Supplemental Report to the Insurance Company Based on The Result of the New Testing and Assessments

The real one-two punch is when you get your own testing, and then give it to your doctor so he or she can write a supplemental report, to go with the Attending Physician Statement he or she already provided. Now that your doctor has more information about your actual functional abilities and expert opinions on your work capacity and employability, he or she can write a much better report in support of your total disability. This one-two punch is the key to preparing the winning claim for disability benefits.

Provide Written Statements From Key Witnesses

In appropriate cases, getting written statements from other people can be very helpful for your claim. People to consider would be family members, co-works, friends or even your boss.

When done right, written statements from others lend credibility to your claims of total disability. These statements are most effective when they focus on specific observations or events witnessed by the person.

For example, I once had a case with a client with severe back pain. When I asked him about specific incidents, he told me about a time when he got stuck half-in and half-out of his car in a driveway. He told me that a woman drove by and later came back and helped him 30 minutes later. She said she had seen him hanging out of the car when she drove by, but didn't realize he was stuck until she was driving back past him 30 minutes later, and noticed he was still in the same position! A written statement from this type of witness is highly effective.

What doesn't work is when family members write letters that really are nothing more than a rant filled with generalizations and irrelevant information. Worse yet are letters with personal attacks directed at the insurance company claims adjuster. Often family members will send these letters to the insurance company without your knowledge, believing they are helping you. Don't allow this to happen to you.

Prepare for Your Interview With the Insurance Company

It is standard practice for insurance companies and disability plan administrators to use a phone interview as part of the initial claims assessment. While you are not obligated to do this type of interview, it makes sense for you to do so. You want to be cooperative and not cause unnecessary problems for the claims adjuster who needs to evaluate your case.

It is important that you treat the phone interview seriously. It is not a time to make jokes or to be overly chatty with the claims adjuster. I am often shocked to see what people say to claims adjusters during these interviews. I have to believe this comes form being nervous or from some underlying embarrassment with describing oneself as being disabled.

You need to prepare yourself to be comfortable talking about your disability in real terms. You need to get comfortable describing your actual abilities, rather than giving "all or nothing" statements, as many people are prone to do.

Here is an example of how all-or-nothing statements can hurt your credibility: You say: "I can't drive any more", when what you should be saying is that "I find it so painful to drive that I only do so on rare occasions." If you say "I can't drive anymore", the insurance company just needs to get video of you driving a car and they can now make you out to be a liar and fraud.

I had another case where my client, before hiring me, gave the following statement: "I can't climb ladders". As you may have already guessed, the insurance company had video of him halfway up a ladder on his house. Of course, the video didn't show him getting down. Trying to later clarify that you were only on the ladder that one time, and your wife and son had to help you down, makes you look like someone making things up. You look like someone caught in a lie, even if you weren't intending to be dishonest when making the statement. This type of thing can ruin your chances of winning, even if you are honest and legitimately disabled.

Precision of language is extremely important whenever you speak with the insurance company. In my experience people are very poor at being precise with language when describing their abilities and limitations. This is why I prepare my clients thoroughly before they speak with the insurance adjuster for the initial interview. I also attend the interview with my client either by phone or in person.

Write A Comprehensive Claim Letter or Legal Brief

The lack of a comprehensive claim letter is one of the biggest weaknesses of most disability claims. A disability claim letter is a ten to twenty page letter that organizes all the information, presents legal authority in your favour, and gives a compelling argument for why the insurance company should approve your disability benefits.

The claim letter is typical of what a personal injury lawyer or disability lawyer would provide to a judge. The purpose of the claim letter or legal brief is to organize the claim information in the most convincing way possible, to influence the insurance adjuster to approve your claim.

To maximize your chances of success, you need to treat your claim like it is going to court. At this stage the claims adjuster is "the judge" of your claim. Contrary to what you may think, claims adjusters are human beings and they appreciate getting claims that are well organized and presented effectively. A well-organized claim makes it much easier for them to approve it. Insurance companies constantly audit their claims adjusters. If your claim is well organized and convincing, they don't have to worry about being second-guessed by their mangers.

CHAPTER 5

Disability Benefits Approved: Know What Happens Next

In this chapter:

- Conditional approvals
- Monthly disability payments
- Offsets and overpayments
- Continuing disability review
- Return to work programs
- Independent medical examinations
- Video and online surveillance

It is always good news when the insurance company approves your application for short- or long-term disability benefits. Most people breathe a sigh of relief and believe the worst is now behind them. In reality, though, most insurance companies do not approve your benefits and then go away. They continue to work hard to justify reasons for stopping payment of benefits. Your insurance company may terminate your benefits after one month, after two months, really at any time.

Conditional Approvals

Over the past number of years, I have noticed a trend where more and more insurance companies are giving *conditional approval* of disability benefits. Sometimes, they tell you they have granted a conditional approval, other times you only find out about it after you sue them and see their internal records. If you are granted *conditional approval* of benefits, you should see this as a major red flag.

By granting *conditional approval*, the insurance company is letting you know that your documents meet the criteria for paying benefits, but they need more time to build a case against you, so they can better justify their decision to deny your benefits. *Conditional approval* just means they are paying benefits now until something else happens in the near future. That something else could be an upcoming doctor's appointment or medical test. It could be a medical report they are waiting to receive from your doctor or their internal medical consultant. It could mean they are waiting for the video and report from the private investigator they hired to investigate or secretly videotape you.

Monthly Disability Payments

Once the insurance company approves your claim, you will start receiving monthly cheques from them for your disability benefit. The amount you receive depends on your specific insurance policy or plan.

Normally you will receive disability payment for being totally unable to work at either your occupation, or any other occupation, or both. However, there are some disability plans that will pay allow you to work and still receive a partial or residual disability payment.

Offsets and Overpayments

All disability insurance policies and plans allow the insurance company or plan administrator to deduct other sources of income from the disability cheque they send you each month.

CPP Disability Benefits

All disability policies and plans have a Canada Pension Plan (CPP) disability offset. This means that if you qualify for CPP disability payments, the amount of the CPP disability payments is "subtracted" from the monthly cheque you get from the disability insurance company.

For example, if the disability insurance company pays you $2,500 per month for your disability insurance benefits, and you get approved for a CPP disability benefit of $1,000 per month, then the insurance company subtracts the $1,000 from the $2,500 it has to pay you. The result is that your monthly income does not go up, you simply get your $2,500 from two sources. You now get a cheque from CPP disability for $1,000 per month and your disability insurance company reduces its cheque to $1,500 per month (down from $2,500 per month).

Please note that some disability policies and plans even allow the insurance company to deduct the CPP disability benefit paid to your children! This practice has been criticized by the CPP administration, but the courts have held it is legal for the insurance company to do this, as long as the right to deduct the child CPP benefit is clearly set out in the insurance policy or benefit plan. Many insurance companies have now backed away from this offset due to criticism, but these offsets still exist in many older policies issued years ago.

Other Possible Offsets

Every disability insurance policy is unique, but other offsets include worker's compensation benefits, retirement benefits, employment severance payments, medical disability payments from other sources, settlements form lawsuits, and income from other sources.

Overpayment Headaches

Many people who are approved for disability insurance benefits will also apply for CPP disability benefits. In fact, most insurance companies and plan administrators will force you to sign forms saying that you agree to apply for CPP disability and to "pay back" the insurance company for any so-called "overpayments" that result from the approval of CPP disability benefits.

You will often be given the choice to either allow the insurance company or plan administrator to estimate the CPP deduction and to start applying it, or you can opt to keep getting the full disability payments and then "pay back" the insurance company later on, if and when you get approved for CPP disability benefits.

In my experience, just about everyone chooses option two, to keep the full disability insurance payment and to "pay back" the insurance company later on if CPP disability is approved.

Once you apply for CPP disability benefits, it can take many months or years to get approved. Once approved though, the CPP disability administration will make a "lump sum" or one-time payment to you for back benefits owing as far back as 14 months before your original application for CPP disability benefits. This can result in you receiving a cheque from CPP disability for $20,000 to $30,000 in addition to the starting of your monthly benefits.

Many people who get the $20,000 or more cheque from CPP disability spend it on paying off bills or loans they got from family members not realizing or remembering that the insurance company views this money as being an "overpayment" that really belongs to them!

Problems arise when you spend the CPP lump sum payment and don't have enough to pay back to the insurance company. This will anger the insurance company or plan administrator and they will either stop payment of your disability insurance benefits, or will put you on a sort of payment-plan, and reduce the amount of your monthly benefit to account for you "paying back" the overpayment.

Insurance companies are aggressive in recovering these overpayments. They will file lawsuits to get a judgment against you. Once they have a judgment, they can send the Sheriff to collect the money from you by freezing your bank accounts or putting liens on your house or other property. I once had a client pass away and the insurance company continued to sue his widow, who had nothing to do with the overpayment problem! I was able to convince the insurance company to take a reduced amount to dismiss its lawsuit, but it shows you the lengths billion-dollar insurance companies will go collect a few thousand dollars from ordinary Canadians.

Why Would I Bother to Apply For CPP Disability if the Insurance Company Gets All The Money?

It is natural for you to question the logic of applying for CPP disability benefits given that your insurance company will get all of the money. Even if you win CPP disability benefits, your monthly income will not increase, the insurance company just gets to pay you less! This leads many people to reasonably ask: why on earth would you want to apply for CPP disability if it only benefits the insurance company?

In my opinion, you should try to win CPP disability benefits even though it appears at first glance that it will only benefit your insurance company. In reality, there are also several benefits to you:

First, winning CPP disability benefits is further validation of your total disability from work and this will make it harder for the insurance company or plan administrator to cut off your disability payments.

Second, if the insurance company does cut off your disability benefits and you later win CPP disability benefits, this puts a lot of pressure on them to either reinstate the disability insurance benefits, or to reach a settlement with you.

Third, CPP disability benefits offer greater piece of mind. Disability insurance companies often cut off payment of benefits unexpectedly for any reason. The CPP administration is not ruthless in this way, so it means that you will be able to rely on still getting the CPP portion of your monthly income, should the disability insurance company cut off your benefits.

Fourth, most disability insurance companies and plan administrators will force you to sign forms saying they have the right to cut off your benefits or reduce your benefit to account for CPP disability, *even if you don't apply for CPP disability and use diligence to try and win payment of those benefits.*

Finally, and perhaps most importantly, **winning CPP disability benefits will actually result in you getting a higher CPP retirement pension down the road.** This is because part of the pension calculation includes "number of years in the workforce". If you don't win CPP disability it will appear that you simply stopped working and didn't contribute to the CPP retirement pension plan. If you win CPP disability benefits, this "not working" penalty would not apply to you, and it will result in a higher retirement pension payment.

Continuing Disability Review

All disability insurance policies make payment of benefits conditional on you proving that you continue to be disabled. This means the insurance company is allowed to continue to monitor your medical condition.

Insurance companies handle this differently. Some will require you or your doctor to fill out monthly update forms. Others will simply call you each month for an update on how you are doing.

Keep in mind that many insurance companies will do undercover surveillance of you during the first two years of your disability. They will compare what you are doing on the videos with what *you say you can do during the phone calls or on the forms.* After watching the videos, the adjuster may call you and work into the conversation whether you can do certain things, with the hope that what you say may be inconsistent with what is on their secret videos of you.

Return to Work Programs

Many disability insurance policies have clauses that require you to attend rehabilitation programs if the insurance company wants you to do so. Sometimes, this will involve you attending a physiotherapy clinic every day for a work-conditioning program. Sometimes, it will involve you working with a vocational counselor.

It is critical you attend these rehabilitation programs and give a full effort, even if you and your doctor believe it is inappropriate and a complete waste of time. The insurance company may even know that this is a complete waste of time, but they require it with the hope that you will refuse to attend or that you attend and are difficult with the rehabilitation workers or that you will not give a full effort.

Why? Because your failure to participate in this type of program will put you in breach of the disability insurance policy, and it is grounds for them to deny your benefits on that basis. In fact, this is the easiest way for an insurance company to build a strong case to deny your claim. I have seen many people fall into this trap, and there is no getting out.

Independent Medical Examinations

All disability insurance policies allow the insurance company to require you to attend medical appointments with a doctor that they choose. These are referred to as "independent medical examinations," or IME's, but in reality they are often anything but "independent."

Again, like with requests to attend rehabilitation programs, you should co-operate with any reasonable request to attend such appointments, even if you and your doctor believe it to be a complete waste of time. The insurance company is hoping that you will refuse to see their doctor, as this will give them strong grounds to deny your application or to stop payment of benefits. You also do not want to get cold feet at the last minute and just not show up for the appointment with their doctor. This doctor will charge a cancellation fee, usually of several thousand dollars. The insurance company will make you pay for this cancellation fee, or they will deduct it from the benefits they are paying you.

There are some grounds for you to refuse to attend a medical appointment with a doctor, for example, if you would have to travel out of province. You are not entitled to refuse to go to the doctor just because you believe the doctor will be biased or unfair. For example, many people will Google the name of the insurance company's doctor and find all kinds of negative comments online from other people involved in disability benefits cases. You cannot refuse to attend just because of these negative comments. In fact, I often tell people it is their lucky day if the insurance company sends them to a biased doctor, as it is less likely that a judge will accept the opinion of that doctor. You should be more worried when the insurance company arranges for you to see a doctor who is regarded as being fair to both sides, as the judge will be more likely to accept that doctor's opinion, and if it goes against you, this is a real problem.

Video and Online Surveillance

The younger you are, and the higher the amount of your disability benefits, the more likely it is that the insurance company will hire a private investigator to secretly videotape you.

Rarely does this type of surveillance produce dramatic evidence that proves you are a liar (unless you actually are a liar). More often, what is seen on the video does not go against what you are saying you are able to do, but it may be vague enough that the insurance company can twist it around to support their decision to deny benefits.

For example, if they see you driving to Tim Horton's every day for a coffee, they will ask why you can't work as a courier. The assertions made by the insurance company are often silly, but that is not the point. The point is that they are looking for anything that superficially supports their decision to terminate payment of benefits.

CHAPTER 6

Disability Benefits Denied: How to Appeal and Win Benefits

In this chapter:

- The denial letter
- Optional internal appeals
- Mandatory internal appeals
- Why most internal appeals fail
- What it takes to win an internal appeal
- Lawsuits

There is a very good chance that the insurance company will deny your application for disability benefits or stop payment of benefits sometime within the first two years. It is important to know this so you can plan ahead and avoid being caught off guard when you get a letter from the insurance company saying they are stopping payment of your benefits.

Once you receive a denial or termination of benefits, your options to appeal will depend on the type of disability plan you have. If you have a typical group disability benefits plan or an individual disability insurance policy, then you have the option to use the insurance company's internal appeal process or you can immediately file a lawsuit against the insurance company.

If your disability benefits are provided through a non-profit disability benefits trust fund, then your appeal options may be more limited. You may not have the option to file a lawsuit right away, or at all.

The Denial Letter

When the insurance company decides to deny your claim or stop payment of benefits, it will send a *denial letter*. You can get this *denial letter* right after you file your claim, before any benefits are paid, or you can get a denial letter after receiving disability payments from the insurance company for months or even years.

The *denial letter* is a very important document in your case going forward. It is important that you keep a clean copy of the letter. Don't mark it up with your own notes and exclamation points! The *denial letter* is important because it sets out the insurance company's reasons for denying your claim (or at least it should). The *denial letter* will usually summarize the medical evidence relied upon and then give reasons for why the evidence was not good enough for the insurance company to approve the claim.

In most cases, the denial letter will also have instructions for how you can appeal the decision. Getting a *denial letter* is a stressful experience; however, don't give up! You can still win payment of benefits by appealing the denial or by filing a lawsuit against the insurance company.

Optional Internal Appeals

All disability insurance policies and plans allow you to appeal a denial of your claim. Insurance companies have different procedures for these appeals, but typically they are unstructured, there are no procedural guidelines, and it simply involves having another person in the insurance company review your claim. You won't be given much guidance on what to do for the appeal other than to send in any "new medical information".

Optional internal appeals mean that you can choose whether to use that process to appeal the decision, or jump straight to filing a lawsuit against the insurance company. Filing a lawsuit is just another way for you to challenge the insurance company's wrongful decision to deny payment of benefits to you.

Mandatory Internal Appeals

With some non-profit disability benefits plans, the internal appeal process is mandatory. With these disability plans, the internal appeal process is much more formalized and usually involves an opportunity to argue your case before a medical review board or internal adjudicator.

It is important to know as soon as possible if your plan has mandatory internal appeals. Some of these plans are designed to take away your right to file a lawsuit. You need to know as soon as possible if you have the right to file a lawsuit if you are unsuccessful at your hearing before the medical review board. It is essential that you get independent advice on your rights and options if you have one of these types of disability plans.

Do not rely on the opinions or advice of co-workers, your union representatives, or your doctors—these people usually mean well but often really don't understand the process and the options open to you.

Why Most Internal Appeals Fail

A disability benefits lawyer from the United States describes having an insurance company deciding an appeal of its own claim denial is like a fox guarding the henhouse. This is one of the reasons internal appeals have such a low success rates.

Early in my career I was a bit more jaded and believed that internal appeals were a complete sham. I believed it was impossible to win because the insurance companies rigged the system that way. Over time, however,

I've softened my thinking on this. I now believe the primary reason for the high failure rate for appeals, is the shoddy approach most people and lawyers take when doing the appeal, and the initial claim before that.

If you are like the vast majority of people handling their own appeal, you will simply do two things. You will ask your doctor to write a new medical report. Then you will write a letter to the insurance company asking them to approve your appeal. There are two problems with this typical approach to internal appeals.

First, simply asking your doctor to write another report, without giving guidance to the doctor, is a waste of time. The doctor simply piles on another report in a format and style that has already proven not to work.

Second, the letters I see people send to insurance companies are often at best ineffective, and at worst can hurt your claim. Writing a letter that is a long rant, or that makes personal attacks on the insurance company is not effective and will reduce your chances of being approved. Also, it is common for people to make threats that they will get a lawyer. While this may work when dealing with ordinary people, a billion-dollar insurance company views they types of threats as silly.

What It Takes To Win An Internal Appeal

It is important to keep in mind that in making an internal appeal you are asking one person in the insurance company to over-rule their co-worker who has already denied your claim. Apart from the insurance company not wanting to pay money to you, there are inter-personal dynamics at work that make it awkward for one employee to over-rule the other employee.

To maximize your chances of success, you need to make it as easy as possible for the appeal reviewer to overturn the claim adjuster's decision and approve your claim. The best way I know to do this is take a very comprehensive approach to the appeal. You want to introduce a lot of new information on the appeal that was not available to the claims adjuster.

This new information can include medical reports, functional capacity testing, witness statements and any other information that supports your claim. You then combine this new information with a comprehensive written appeal brief, with legal arguments explaining why the reasons given for denial no longer apply.

With all of this new information and the appeal brief, you make it much easier for the person handling the appeal to approve your claim. You allow the original claims handler to save face because he or she can say: "Well if I had all that information, I would have approve the claim too!"

Finally, insurance companies also audit and monitor the decisions of the appeal reviewers, just as they do with the claims adjusters. Put yourself in the shoes of the person doing the appeal review. If the reviewer grants appeals that are then overturned by the insurance company auditors, it will damage his or her career within the company. This is why – when in doubt – appeal reviewers default to denying your appeal. They won't get in trouble for <u>denying</u> a borderline appeal, but will absolutely get reprimanded for <u>approving</u> a borderline appeal.

Your job is to make sure your appeal is not on the borderline. You have to make sure your appeal is not simply a repackaging of the same information that was given to the claims adjuster.

So what does it take to prepare a "winning" appeal? Following is the process we use at Resolute Legal when preparing internal appeals for our clients. While no method can guarantee you will win in all cases, we are confident our approach gives you the best possible chance of success:

Plan The Perfect Strategy

There is no one-size-fits-all appeal. You need to create a unique strategy for the appeal based on three factors: 1) your occupation; 2) your illness; and 3) the insurance company you are dealing with. Creating a strategy requires extensive experience with the claims process and knowledge of any peculiarities of the insurance company you are dealing with. You can't learn this type of knowledge from reading a book like this. You would need to work with a lawyer experienced with disability insurance benefits claims.

Get a Copy of the Insurance Company's Complete File

You won't maximize your chances of success at an internal appeal unless you get your hands on the insurance company's complete claims file. Specifically, you want to see copies of the reports from the behind-the-scenes doctors. These reports are often the basis for the claim adjuster's denial of your claim.

If you can get copies of those medical reports of the behind-the-scenes doctors, then you can then get your own doctors to poke holes in what those other doctors have said. This is often the most effective way to take the legs out from under the insurance company's denial of your claim.

There is one problem with this approach. The insurance company has no legal obligation to give you a complete copy of its claims file at the internal appeals stage. You may have to hire a lawyer to get the claim file.

Get the Insurance Company to Give Detailed Reasons for the Denial

Many insurance companies will send denial letters with very vague reasons for the denial. If you want to maximize your chances of success, you need to get the insurance company to give detailed reasons for why it denied your claim.

Insurance companies like to keep things vague. You want to make them commit to specific reasons and evidence for the denial. Then you can focus your attack on undercutting those specific reasons and evidence. You do this by getting any missing information or medical opinions that would address all the reasons given in the denial letter. Then when filing your appeal brief you can go though the reasons one-by-one and show why they are no longer valid given the new information and medical reports you are providing. The approach is highly effective.

Get Your Own Testing and Assessments to Verify Your Medical Condition or Disability

If you have not already gotten your own testing and assessments done at the initial claim stage, the appeal stage is the ideal time to do it. The results of new testing and assessments are just the sort of thing the appeal reviewer needs to allow your appeal and overturn the denial.

The type of assessment or testing that would maximize your chances of success needs to be determined on a case-by-case basis. You need to take into account your occupation, your medical condition, existing medical reports, *and the insurance company's reasons for denial given in the denial letter.*

Examples of tests and assessments include, functional capacity evaluations, functional abilities assessments, neuropsychological testing, transferable skills assessments, examinations by specialist physicians and vocational expert assessments.

These assessments are necessary because they provide direct opinions on your physical and mental abilities from people who are qualified to give such opinions. Contrary to what you may believe, doctors are really not qualified to give opinions on your functional abilities or ability to work at a particular job.

The key to winning your disability claim is to present overwhelming evidence of disability. In many cases, it is nearly impossible to build overwhelming evidence without paying for your own medical testing and assessments.

The difficulty with getting your own testing and assessments is that you have to pay for them yourself. These tests usually cost into the thousands of dollars. Unfortunately, Medicare does not cover these tests and assessments because they are not essential to your medical care. Disability lawyers will typically pay the cost of these assessments when your case is at the lawsuit stage; however, at the internal appeals stage you would likely have to pay for these tests and assessment out of your own pocket.

Get Your Doctor to Write a Supplemental Report

The appeal represents a new opportunity to get a much better report from your doctor. You should not get your doctor to write a supplemental report until you have gotten the results of your additional testing and a complete copy of the insurance company's claims file.

You maximize the impact of your doctor's report by having him or her comment on the results of any new testing you had done, and also the opinions given by the insurance company's behind-the-scenes doctors.

The opinions of the behind-the-scenes doctors are usually one of the key reasons your claim was denied. Armed with the new testing you had done, and seeing exactly what the other doctors wrote in your claim file, your doctor is now in a much better position to give a rebuttal of the opinions given by the insurance company's behind-the-scenes doctors.

Provide Written Statements from Key Witnesses

In appropriate cases, getting written statements from other people can help you win payment of disability benefits. You should consider getting statements from family members, co-works, friends or even your boss.

When done right, written statements from others lends credibility to your claim of total disability. These statements are most effective when they focus on specific observations or events.

For example, I once had a case with a client with severe back pain. When asking him about specific incidents he told me about a time when he got stuck half-in and half-out of his car in a driveway. He told me that a lady drove by and later came back and helped him 30 minutes later. She said she had seen him hanging out of the car when she drove by, but didn't realize he was stuck until she was driving back by him 30 minutes later! A written statement from this type of witness is highly effective.

What doesn't work is when family members write letters that really are nothing more than a rant filled with generalizations and irrelevant information. Worse yet are letters directing personal attacks against the claims representatives. Often family members will send these letters to the insurance company without your knowledge, believing they are helping you. Don't allow this to happen to you.

Prepare a Comprehensive Written Statement

By the internal appeals stage, the insurance company will usually have lots of information about you. This information would come from the initial claim forms you provided. From the medical reports and records you provided. And from the many phone conversations you had with the claims adjusters. While the insurance may have a lot of information, it does not mean that they have the complete picture of your situation.

By providing a detailed written statement you can make sure the appeal reviewer has a complete understanding of your situation. For example, one of the biggest areas of misunderstanding is *your actual job demands and duties*. If you did the "bare minimum" approach to your initial claim, as described earlier in this book, then it is quite possible there is misleading information about your employment and job duties. If you have not seen the report your employer provided, then you need to get a copy of the Employer's Report and review it. If the Employer's Report is not one hundred percent accurate, you can address each of the problems or issues in your written statement.

For your written statement to be effective, it is critical that it does not have an angry tone or come off as a rant. This statement is not the appropriate time to vent your frustrations with the insurance company, no matter how valid those frustrations may be. It is also not the time to beg and plead for the sympathies of the appeal reviewer. He or she may have great sympathy for your situation, but would get fired for approving a claim based only on that type of evidence!

Your statement needs to provide a convincing narrative about your disability. You need to go into great detail about the progression of your disability in the years leading up to your last day of work. It needs to describe your job duties and then explain how your disability interfered with your ability to do those duties. You need to explain why you could work the day before you stopped working, but not afterwards. You need to explain why your medical condition is disabling for you, but not for many other people with the same medical diagnosis. You should discuss what a typical day looks like for you. You need to explain the steps you have taken to get better and to try and remain at work.

One word of caution when preparing a detailed statement is that you should also indicate how long it took you to prepare it and if you had help from other people. Insurance companies will argue that the fact you could prepare such a detailed statement demonstrates your capacity to work!

For maximum impact you can give your written statement as a sworn affidavit. This means you have sworn that what you have written is the truth. This is no different than you swearing to tell the truth when you testify in court. It is a crime to tell lies when under oath, so this means the insurance company will put much more stock in what you have said.

Write a Comprehensive Appeal Brief

The lack of a comprehensive appeal brief is one of the biggest weaknesses of most internal appeals. An appeal brief is a ten to twenty page letter that organizes all the information, presents legal authority in your favour, and gives a compelling argument for why the insurance company should approve your disability benefits. It attaches all the critical documents and evidence, so the person reviewing it will have all the information in one place.

The appeal brief is typical of what lawyers would provide to a judge in a lawsuit. The purpose of the appeal brief is to organize the case information in the most convincing way possible, to influence the appeal reviewer to rule in your favor.

For maximum effect, your appeal brief should address each of the reasons given for the denial. One-by-one, you need to discuss why each reason was deficient, or how it is no longer valid given the new information and evidence attached to the appeal brief.

Contrary to what you may think, appeal reviewers appreciate it when they get an appeal that is well organized and effectively presented. You make the appeal review's job easier, because he or she can approve your claim with confidence, knowing the decision to do so won't be criticized or second-guessed by others in the insurance company.

Lawsuits

You can file a lawsuit to enforce your right to disability benefits under an insurance policy or plan. Insurance is regulated on a province-by-province basis, so the lawsuit is filed in the Superior Court of your province. The Superior Courts go by different names depending on your province; two examples are the Court of Queen's Bench and the Supreme Court, but there are others.

You engage the court process by filing a lawsuit against the insurance company for wrongful denial of disability benefits. There certain procedures that must be done, but basically the purpose of filing a lawsuit is so you can get a hearing before a judge or jury, who will decide your case. The decision of the judge or jury is legally binding on both you and the insurance company.

Can I File a Lawsuit?

The vast majority of people denied disability insurance benefits have the right to file a lawsuit against the insurance company. There are exceptions. Some disability plans go to great lengths to remove your right to use the court system.

If your disability benefits are paid though a non-profit disability plan, then it's possible you might not have the right to bring a lawsuit. The only way to know for sure is to have a disability benefits lawyer review your policy.

When Can I File A Lawsuit?

You can file a lawsuit as soon as the insurance company denies your claim or stops payment of benefits. In most cases you don't have to do the internal appeals before filing a lawsuit. There are some exceptions to this general rule, so you should have a disability benefits lawyer review your policy to know for sure.

Who is the Lawsuit Against?

In most cases, your lawsuit is against your the insurance company. In some cases, the insurance company is only administering the disability plan on behalf your employer or not-profit entity. If that applies to you, then your lawsuit would be against your employer or the non-profit entity. This is an area of confusion for many people, including less experienced lawyers.

Where is My Lawsuit Filed?

Insurance is regulated on a province-by-province basis, so your lawsuit should normally be filed in the province or territory where you live. Even if you moved to another province after your benefits have terminated, courts will normally allow you to file the lawsuit where you live. Each province is called a "jurisdiction" because it has its own court system.

While courts will usually allow you to file the lawsuit where you live, the law of another province may apply to your case. Since insurance companies are national companies, they will sometimes put clauses in the insurance policy that say the law of a certain province will apply, regardless of where the lawsuit is filed.

For example, many insurance companies are headquartered in Ontario. It it is common to see a clause in the insurance policy that says: "the law of Ontario shall apply to disputes arising under this policy". So in these situations, you can file your lawsuit in New Brunswick, and the New Brunswick Courts would handle it, but the lawyers and judge would need to apply the insurance laws from Ontario, as opposed to the insurance laws of New Brunswick. This is not as big a deal as it may seem, but it is a detail often overlooked by inexperienced lawyers handling disability insurance lawsuits.

What Can I Sue For?

Lawsuits allow you get compensation for many things that are not otherwise available to you with internal appeals. When you do an internal appeal, the only thing you can win is payment of back benefits owed and resumption of monthly payments going forward.

On the other hand, when you file a lawsuit you can get compensation for some or all of the following things:

- Payment of past benefits owing, plus interest
- Compensation for mental distress caused by the denial
- Compensation for damage done to your credit rating
- Compensation for any losses you suffered from selling your house for less than market value due to financial distress
- Pension losses suffered due to the denial of benefits
- Financial losses arising from the loss of your group medical plan that was tied to the approval of disability benefits
- Punitive damages awarded to punish the insurance company for despicable behavior

How Long Do I Have to File the Lawsuit?

There are strict deadlines for starting your lawsuit. If you don't file the lawsuit before the deadline, then your will lose your right to do so, even if your are truly disabled and would have won in court.

There is no standard deadline for filing a lawsuit. The time available to file a lawsuit will normally be stated in your insurance policy or plan. If your insurance policy or plan does not give a deadline for filing a lawsuit, then you would have to meet the deadlines in the *Insurance Act* or *Statute of Limitations* of your province or territory.

Many people contact me after their deadline to file a lawsuit has passed. Unfortunately, this happens all the time. Usually because the person was not aware they had a right to bring a lawsuit. People think the internal appeal was the final decision on their case. I have even experienced a situation where a person stayed in the internal appeals stage so long (well over a year) that he missed the deadline to file a lawsuit. Or at least that was the position his insurance company took when we sued them.

What Do I Have to Prove to Win a Lawsuit?

As the person filing a lawsuit, you are called "the Plaintiff". This is just a technical term used by the court system. In Canada, the plaintiff always has the burden of proof in court. This means that the judge or jury's default position is that you are not disabled. For them to move off of this default position, you must convince them that it is "more likely than not" that you are disabled as defined by your insurance policy. Technically speaking, the insurance company doesn't have to do anything to win. If you don't convince the judge or jury that it is more likely than not that you are disabled, then they will stay at the default position that you are not disabled, and you will lose.

To prove your case, you must present evidence that is admissible in court. I emphasize "admissible in court" because you might know something to be true, but if you can't prove it using evidence that is admissible in court, then you have no chance of the judge or jury ruling in your favour. This is why trials are not always about the truth, but merely what you can prove in court.

I strongly discourage your from trying to represent yourself in a lawsuit. This is a recipe for disaster. For example, I once represented a lawyer who was making a disability claim. He started the lawsuit on his own and was trying to represent himself. He had experience with civil litigation so he thought he could do it. He made a real mess of things, some of which I was unable to undo. Disability insurance law is a very specialized area of law. Very few lawyers in Canada have developed a high level of competence and expertise in disability insurance claims.

What Are the Possible Outcomes of a Lawsuit?

When doing a lawsuit for wrongful denial of disability insurance benefits, the possible outcomes, depending on the strength of your case, will be as follows:

- **Reinstatement:** At any time during the lawsuit the insurance company can change its mind and reinstate your benefits. They will make a one-time payment for the back benefits owing and then start paying you each month going forward.
- **Settlement:** At any time during the lawsuit, you and the insurance company can settle the case. These settlements are usually for a one-time payment in exchange for you signing off on any future rights under the policy. Such settlements normally include full payment of all back benefits owing plus a payment representing a percentage of the future benefits owing under the policy. The size of the percentage of future benefits will depend on the insurance company's perception of how likely you would be to win, if the case went to trial.
- **Motion for Summary Judgment:** Either side can ask a motions judge to make a final decision on your case before the case goes to

trial. This usually happens when the insurance company brings a motion for summary judgment when it believes you have missed a deadline to file the lawsuit, or are not eligible for disability benefits for some other reason. If the insurance company wins this motion, your lawsuit is dismissed, and you lose your claim.

- **Winning at Trial before a Judge or Jury:** If the insurance company does not reinstate your benefits, and there is no out-of-court settlement, then your case will go to trial before a judge-alone or a jury. When that happens either the judge or the jury will make the final decision on whether the insurance company must pay benefits to you. The judge and jury can also force the insurance company to pay other compensation to you for mental distress, punitive damages, or for other financial losses you have suffered because of the wrongful denial of benefits. If you win, the court will order the insurance company to pay a portion of the legal fees charged by your lawyers and any litigation expenses paid by you or your lawyers.

- **Losing at Trial Before a Judge or Jury:** If you lose at trial, then obviously the insurance company does not have to pay you any compensation. If you have a contingency fee agreement with your lawyer, then you won't have to pay your own lawyers. While you may not have to pay your own lawyers, the court will order you to pay "costs" to the insurance company, which will be portion of the insurance company's legal fees and litigation expenses in defending against your lawsuit. You have control over this risk of loss because often the insurance company will have made settlement offers to you up to the time of trial. You will usually have the opportunity to avoid the risk of losing at trial by reaching an out-of-court settlement with the insurance company.

CHAPTER 7

Compensation, Settlements, and Court Verdicts

In this chapter:

- What is a settlement?
- How to determine the settlement value of your case?
- What are the risks of going to trial?

What Is a Settlement?

In the context of disability benefits claims, a settlement means that you and the insurance company reach an agreement to resolve your claim for benefits. If you reach a settlement after filing your lawsuit, it usually involves the insurance company agreeing to pay a specific amount of money to you in exchange for you agreeing to dismiss your lawsuit.

There are two types of settlements in disability insurance disputes. In one type of settlement, the insurance company agrees to make a one-time payment to you in exchange for you dismissing your lawsuit and releasing them from any liability to pay you anything in the future. In the second type of settlement, you agree to dismiss your lawsuit and release the insurance company from any future claims for mental distress or punitive damages *in exchange for the insurance company restarting your monthly payments and paying you for the back benefits it owes you, with interest.*

How to Determine the Settlement Value of Your Case?

Keep in mind that the *settlement value* of your case is whatever the insurance company is willing to pay. If they don't make an offer to pay some amount of money, your case can't settle out of court. What the insurance company is willing to pay for a settlement is based on a number of factors, including the following:

- the value of your past benefits owed
- the present value of your future benefits
- the value of other benefits provided under policy
- the insurance company's appreciation of its own risks of losing at trial
- the insurance company's appreciation of its own risk of exposure to extra contractual damages at trial (i.e., punitive damages, mental distress damages)
- the insurance company's impression about the quality of your lawyer
- how close your case is to trial

Your lawyer's job is to make sure the insurance company offers you the entire amount it is willing to pay for an out of court settlement. You don't want to accept less than the maximum amount they are willing to pay. The only way your lawyer can do this is to move your case toward trial and to do things to *increase* the insurance company's appreciation of its own risks of losing the case at trial.

What Are the Risks of Going to Trial?

Do not make the mistake of believing your case is a "sure thing" if you go to court. I can assure you there are no sure bets when it comes to litigation. I have found this is one of the most difficult things for people to understand. *Most people do not appreciate how the courts really work and how judges and juries make decisions.*

You know the "truth" of your case, but a judge or jury will not decide your case based on the truth as you know it; rather, *judges and juries are required by law to make decisions based only on evidence that is admissible at trial, and what can be proven in court.* Often things can be true, but difficult to prove at court.

Canadian Provinces all have the "loser pays" rule for lawsuits. This means that in any lawsuit, the unsuccessful side must pay a portion of the legal expenses of the successful side. For example, if you go to court and win, the insurance company must pay a portion of your legal expenses (legal fees and disbursements), in addition to paying your benefits owed under the insurance policy. The reverse is also true. If you go to court and lose, then the court will order you to pay a portion of the insurance company's legal fees and expenses.

CHAPTER 8

Lawyers and Legal Fees

In this chapter:

- Do I need a lawyer?
- What can a lawyer do for me?
- When is the best time to hire a lawyer?
- What are typical lawyer fees and prices?

Do I Need a Lawyer?

This is a fair question. In theory, insurance claims are designed to be straightforward and easy. The claims adjuster is supposed to help you fill out forms to apply for benefits. They are supposed to tell you want information they need to approve the claim.

The reality, however, is that insurance companies don't play fairly. Some insurance companies will deny claims they know they should pay, unless the claim is so well put together that it creates overwhelming evidence in favour of approval. Most people cannot put together an overwhelming claim without the help of a lawyer who is experienced in long-term disability benefits cases.

What Can a Lawyer Do for Me?

Following is a list of the things that a lawyer can do for you (not all of these things will need to be done in all cases):

- interview you to understand your situation
- educate you about disability benefits claims
- prepare a strategy to maximize your chances of success
- gather documents needed for your application and case, including important medical records
- help you get a copy of your benefits booklet and explain the specific benefits to which you are entitled
- help prepare your application for short-term and long-term disability benefits
- help you prepare a comprehensive written statement that will give the insurance company a better understanding of your situation
- identify and anticipate the key issues in your case that the insurance company will try to take advantage of
- write to your doctor to make sure he or she provides the kind of information that will make it harder for the insurance company to deny your application
- act as a buffer between you and the insurance company; all letters and documents go through the lawyer
- watch the insurance company to prevent them from setting any traps for you or from using dirty tricks on you
- help you prepare documents for internal appeals
- represent you at medical board hearings
- file a lawsuit on your behalf
- represent you in litigation and at trial
- negotiate a settlement with the insurance company

When Is the Best Time to Hire a Lawyer?

This may surprise you, but the best time to consult a lawyer is before you stop working. Having a lawyer help you at this early stage gives you the best possible chance winning. You can avoid making the common mistakes that can haunt you throughout your case. Many people don't appreciate how easy it is for an honest and well-meaning person "screw up" a winnable case. If you get a lawyer involved too late, you severely handicap the lawyer's ability to fix the mistakes.

What Are Typical Lawyers' Fees and Prices?

There are no standard legal fees or prices for disability insurance cases. Lawyers charge different fees and prices depending on what you are hiring them to do (e.g., initial claim, internal appeals, or lawsuit).

The legal fee arrangements, and the amounts you have to pay, will normally be different depending on who bears the financial risk of losing the case, you or the lawyer. When you bear the risk of losing, you have to pay a legal fee regardless if you win or lose. When the lawyer bears the risk, it means you will only have to pay the lawyer if he wins your case.

Following is a summary of different fee arrangements you may encounter when hiring a lawyer for a disability benefits case:

Paying the Lawyer By-The-Hour

Many lawyers will offer to represent you on an hourly-rate basis. They quote you an hourly rate and then bill you based on the time worked. Usually in six minute increments. Under this arrangement, the lawyer gets paid, win or lose. Therefore, you bear the risk of losing; in that you pay the legal fees regardless if you win or lose.

Paying by the hour is rarely in your interests. Most often you end up paying for the lawyer's time spent doing useless work, or work that had no real chance of success. Paying by the hour can add up quickly as most lawyers will charge hourly rates well in excess of one hundred dollars per hour.

Be extremely cautious when a lawyer offers to handle your disability case on an hourly rate basis. This is often a sign of a lawyer who is inexperienced with disability insurance cases. You are much better off to negotiate a flat rate for work to be done. Inexperienced lawyers may be unwilling to do this because they really don't know what the work will involve. They are learning as they go along. You may end up wasting a lot of money without advancing your case.

With a pay-by-the-hour fee arrangement, the lawyer has no financial incentive to win or to be as productive as possible. Oddly, pay-by-the hour arrangements reward lawyers who are unproductive, waste time and drag things out as long as possible.

Flat Rate Billing

With flat rate billing, you pay a pre-determined fee for the lawyer to give a specific service. For example, a lawyer may offer you a flat rate of $3,000 to prepare and file your application for disability benefits. With flat rate billing you bear the risk of loss, because you pay the fee regardless of whether you win or lose the disability claim. Flat rate billing removes the incentive for the lawyer to be unproductive or to drag things out. The downside is that the lawyer has no financial incentive to win the claim because they get paid the same amount of money, win or lose.

Flat Rate Billing With Success Payment

By including a success payment as part of the fee, you begin to share the risk of loss with the lawyer. With this type of arrangement you pay an agreed upon fee (win or lose), with an additional agreed upon fee to be paid only if the lawyer wins. This type of arrangement allows you to negotiate a lower up-front fee and shift the majority of the fee to a success payment. For example, a lawyer might agree to prepare and file your initial application for a flat fee of $1,000 with a success payment of $4,000. Under this arrangement the lawyer has a financial incentive to win because he or she gets paid much more for winning.

Contingency Fee Billing

Contingency fee billing arrangements are the last type of payment arrangement lawyers will use in disability insurance cases. Contingency fee agreements are often referred to as no-win, no-fee agreements. With these agreements, the payment of legal fees is one hundred percent conditional upon the lawyer being successful.

If your lawyer doesn't win payment of disability benefits, then you don't have to pay any legal fee. Lawyers will agree to take on this risk, but only if the potential legal fee is increased in direct proportion to the amount of financial recovery. Legal fees are calculated as a percentage of the total settlement or money recovered from the insurance company. These percentages usually run in the range of 20-30% depending on a number of factors.

With this arrangement the lawyer's legal fee is indexed to the financial recovery. This means that your legal fee will never be more than the recovery no matter how little, or how much, the lawyer recovers for you.

With contingency fee agreements, some lawyers will also agree to take on the risk of payment for the expenses necessary to run the case. These expenses include things like paying for copies of medical records, court filing fees, paying for additional assessments and testing. Expenses on a disability case can easily be several thousand dollars and tens of thousands of dollars if your case goes to a trial. The lawyer would only get paid back for these expenses if he or she wins. Not all lawyers will agree to take-on this additional risk.

With contingency agreements, the lawyer has the strongest possible financial incentive to win – otherwise, not only will he not get paid, he will often lose money because he will not get paid back for money spent on the above-mentioned legal expenses.

NOTES

NOTES

NOTES

NOTES